D0577510

CALGARY PUBLIC LIBRARY

JUN - 2012

To my mother and father, who always encouraged me to be Jennifer,
and to Lena for her devotion and talents

JENNIFER POST PURE SPACE

ELEGANT MINIMALISM

BY **ANNA KASABIAN**   FOREWORD BY **PAIGE RENSE**

RIZZOLI
NEW YORK

New York · Paris · London · Milan

CONTENTS

FOREWORD BY PAIGE RENSE

Jennifer Post seemed to appear from outer space.

One day in my AD office I was going through the latest submissions with my key staff. We did this review every ten days or so. This routine allowed us to keep up with the two-thousand-plus submissions that came to us each year. About halfway through the lineup of images from international architects and interior designers as well as homeowners, we saw the work of Jennifer Post for the first time. There she was in all her white, minimalist glory.

"Who did this?" we asked each other. Executive editor Margaret Dunne replied, "The name is Jennifer Post." "I've never heard of her," said James Huntington, photography director. "Neither have I," my executive assistant, Beverly Montgomery, agreed.

We wanted to find out about her because we were always happy to discover a talent unknown to us. The photographs from Jennifer Post showed us a thoroughly professional understanding of space, lighting, and composition. Her work had the purity of a nun. All-encompassing white, punctuated with classic furniture and carefully chosen artwork.

It was and is her signature design. She believed in it and has stuck to her pearl-handled guns. If a prospective client wants a different look, she gracefully declines.

When her work was first published in AD, the reaction from our readers was entirely positive. One quote is a good example. "Jennifer Post's work is very spare, almost Spartan, but never cold and sterile."

We agreed and included her work in our coveted AD 100 list of professional architects and interior designers around the world, and in our world.

Jennifer Post, the designer from outer space, turned out to be a great talent with inner space.

My first contact with Jennifer Post came more than ten years ago, when I was writing *East Coast Rooms*, which highlighted the top designers and architects on the East Coast. I was looking for a designer immersed in classical contemporary design and someone who possessed a rock-solid design philosophy. This was Jennifer then, and now.

In all this time she has never wavered from her less-is-more, uncluttered design posture that is rooted in bringing in the light of day with unencumbered views, allowing her to transform homes into peaceful, ethereal sanctuaries.

No matter who her clients are—families, professionals, or Hollywood luminaries—they share the common goal to live in an elegant, modern, high-function home anchored in serenity. Jennifer's projects take her across the globe, and her work is all encompassing: from architectural design to interior design, custom furnishings, commissioned art, and landscape design. She designs nearly all of the rugs and furniture for her clients' homes. And with all this has come both national and international recognition and honors. The time was right to embark on this monograph that defines Jennifer Post.

She will tell you in no uncertain terms that she is a perfectionist and her projects are immaculately conceived, detailed, and constructed. Those who continue to inspire her are architects Santiago Calatrava and Renzo Piano, artists Louise Nevelson and Alberto Giacometti, and designer Alberto Pinto. Look at their work and Jennifer's, and you can clearly see why.

Jennifer is known to personally sketch, draw, and document all the design details of her projects, and her firm provides comprehensive construction management under her watchful, meticulous eye. Jennifer's study of architectural principles and her fine arts background combine for an approach that treats each of her commissions like artwork.

Making spaces perfect goes back to her childhood in Ohio, where she preferred building blocks, drawing, and painting to dolls or dress-up games. She was only eight years old when she pulled her red wagon around the neighborhood looking to rearrange people's rooms. And so began the Post style.

Later, enamored with theater design, she studied at the University of Cincinnati and went on to receive an MFA from Michigan State. She then pursued postgraduate work in fine arts and theater design at the University of London. It was this experience that clarified the distinct artistic relationship between stage design and home design: "as on the stage, when you enter someone's home, the architecture and design should be seamless," says Jennifer.

Very early in her career, Jennifer worked as an art director in advertising and interned at a few architectural firms. When her path to designing interiors crystallized, she opened her own design studio out of a barn she renovated in the Hamptons. Today, with an office in Manhattan and satellite offices in Miami and Los Angeles, she looks to her own serene home in Manhattan to replenish her creative juices (see pages 202–11).

Her work emphasizes clear spatial organization on a primary axis, and adheres to strict rules of balance, continuity, and clarity of forms. When she introduces color or luxurious textures, they are in moderation and always come with a very specific purpose. She is the first to tell you that every design component in her work comes from a plan.

The eighteen projects on these pages span nineteen years of Jennifer Post's elegant minimalism from coast to coast. "Showcasing this body of work represents countless hours of my passion for creative expression," says the designer. "It takes me back, page by page, to each and every moment of seeing my inspirations turned reality: a concept turned into a home, and a client so pleased to live there."

This 1960s ranch perched in the Doheny Estates of West Los Angeles went far beyond the expected spatial solutions. Jennifer's plans for the architecture, interior design, and landscape design took this 3,500-square-foot space to a provocative place, opening it up and ultimately transforming it from the classic ranch it had been. This suited her client, a celebrity who wanted to feel calmed when she came here to hide from the clamor of public life. It also answered her client's wish for a space that would feel welcoming to guests and offer a variety of spaces to move about, relax, and dine inside and out.

"It took a year to create, but as soon as I walked in the front door I knew what I wanted to do. I did one schematic and focused on making this so, so precise," Jennifer says.

In place of the ranch house came a new layout, lots of glass, a formal entranceway, a great room for indoor entertaining, long, wide hallways, a gallery that unfolded new views, a master suite with a huge walk-in closet, and a serene home office.

The palette is quiet and subdued; the space light with panels of glass charting the sun, blue sky, and all that Jennifer wove into the newly sculpted landscape.

She designed and constructed an eighty-foot raised terrace—a stunning outdoor room complete with a dining area overlooking a new outdoor pool as well as a massive, multi-layered fireplace with ribbons of fire. "It's the perfect place for her to have dinner parties, watch the sun set or the stars emerge."

Of the project Jennifer notes, "This was an exquisite journey. I had a great client who participated in the design, but she always trusted me on the final decision. It was a 'small' big project because it is only 3,500 square feet, yet it is a big statement in that amount of space."

Opposite: A trio of Ralph Lauren hurricane lanterns guides our steps across smooth cut stones that float over a water pool. The din of the day is easily left behind.
Following pages: In classic Post white, the walls and overhead structure tent the entrance and take our eye to the entryway and beyond to Clayton Rabo's *Thinking*.

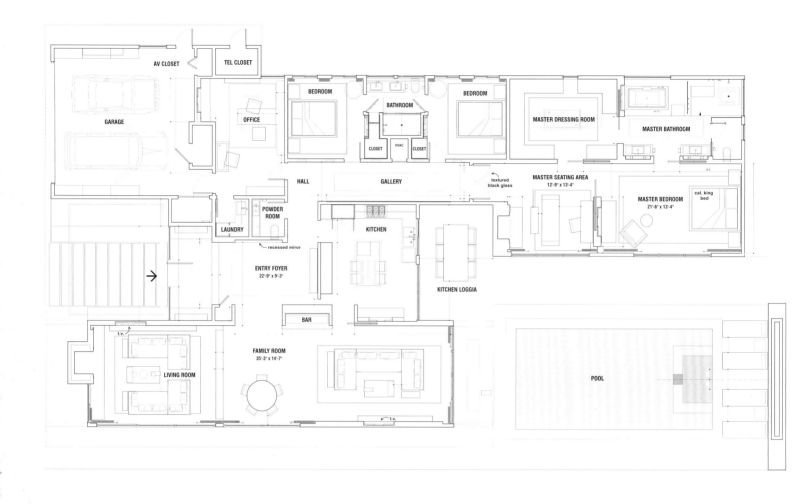

AV CLOSET

TEL CLOSET

GARAGE

OFFICE

BEDROOM

BATHROOM

BEDROOM

MASTER DRESSING ROOM

MASTER BATHROOM

CLOSET HVAC CLOSET

HALL

GALLERY

textured black glass

MASTER SEATING AREA
12'-9" x 13'-4"

cal. king bed

MASTER BEDROOM
21'-6" x 13'-4"

POWDER ROOM

LAUNDRY

recessed mirror

KITCHEN

ENTRY FOYER
22'-9" x 9'-3"

KITCHEN LOGGIA

t.v.

BAR

FAMILY ROOM
35'-3" x 14'-7"

POOL

LIVING ROOM

t.v.

Opposite: The wide, mirrored hall leading to the dressing room and master bedroom cleverly houses closets, flush to the wall, that lead to guest bedrooms. There is no hardware to disrupt the purity of the architecture. Muted sand, cream, and blonde-toned furnishings ahead provide a warm glow while distinguishing the spaces.

Above: Jennifer uses fabric color and furnishing placement to create two "rooms" for entertaining. The marble *Lady Mamba*, a creation of Italian sculptor Mauro Mori, further defines the two areas. Low Minotti seating accentuates the openness of the room, and the walls of glass introduce the landscape as living art on three sides.

Above: *Conversation*, by Kari Taylor, introduces an earthy, warm palette into this snow-white study with a floor-to-ceiling view of greenery. **Following pages:** Here is the ultimate feminine dressing room, with the sexy temptress Marilyn, shades of white, a lounge chair by Ligne Roset, and a dressing table by J. Robert Scott.

Above and opposite: Glass tiles and butter-hued limestone wrap this luxuriously spacious walk-in shower. Park-like views to the outdoors, framed in oversized glass panels, encourage long stays here, or sinking into the whirlpool for a relaxing soak. What appears to be a mirror over the tub is actually a television set.

Following pages: Here we see the full view of the highly textured landscape that frames the extra-deep tub. Hardware is slim, cut like gemstones, and like all other water works, sits quietly in the background. The glass tile wrapping the walls functions like a cool-to-the-touch, stone fabric that accentuates the spa-like atmosphere.

Above and opposite: Outdoor rooms are designated via furnishings and open walls, perched atop Basaltina Gray stone. Dining table and chairs are by David Sutherland.

Following pages: The pool provides a focal point for public and private rooms. Whether gray sky or blue, this view holds the peacefulness of the place in check.

COLUMBUS CIRCLE PARIS MEETS PURE

From the sixty-seventh floor of these twin towering spikes of glass and steel is a Google Earth view of Manhattan, from one end to another. The graceful Columbus Circle towers, the creation of architectural firm Skidmore, Owings & Merrill, are poignant reminders, says Jennifer, of America's enduring spirit. For those who live here, it is a luxurious escape.

Her client, a renowned eye surgeon, keeps the kind of schedule that has him moving from planes to operating rooms all over the world with the frequency of a commercial pilot. When he and his wife stop over in New York at this 2,300-square-foot pied-à-terre, it is for rest, a little work, and dinner parties, often with royalty.

His call to Jennifer was prompted by her style: the absolute calm that emotes from her rooms. He was also drawn to the perfectionism that is required to execute these concepts.

The first, and worst, architectural sin of this newly constructed space was that the views of Central Park were obliterated by a wall upon entering. But there were many more walls that had to come down. So down to the studs Jennifer went. The enclosed kitchen, no more. The living room wall, the bedroom walls—gone. All of those light-blocking fortresses were eliminated, allowing the rooms to unfold, one into another. When Jennifer's work was complete, all rooms shared a panoramic view of the park. Now it all made architectural sense: a man known around the world for bringing the light of day to his patients would have a constant reminder of his life's work.

The study and living room, a gorgeous stretch of forty-five feet, are now referred to as the great room. A freestanding glass panel separates the two rooms. Floors are now paths of Carrera marble. Where a bit of warmth is needed underfoot, big squares of handmade rugs from Nepal have been introduced.

Nearly all the circa-1940s furnishings were imported from Paris. Jennifer designed the dining room table, and custom millwork throughout the apartment cleverly makes the necessities of daily life disappear. Her palette borrows shades of blue from the morning sky in Manhattan and a bit of lavender that recalls the painterly hue that can wash across the clouds at dusk.

"This is a modern, intellectual home. It is as comfortable to be here in your sweats as it is to have a candlelit dinner party," Jennifer says.

Opposite: When the front door opens, the wide, marble-floored gallery opens into light-filled space. **Following pages:** Low, sculpted living room furnishings put views center stage. The 1960s European couch and chairs, in the style of Nana Dietzel, are refinished with custom details; the low John Boone table is metal and glass.

Above: A sculpture, *Explosion* from Kamp Studios, introduces a bit of whimsy and texture to the glass-like surfaces. Black sculpted rocks guide us to other rooms.

Above: Punctuating a turn is a bronze sculpture aptly titled *Expecting* by Dimitry German. Seamless doors hide closets, the washer and dryer, and other necessities of life.

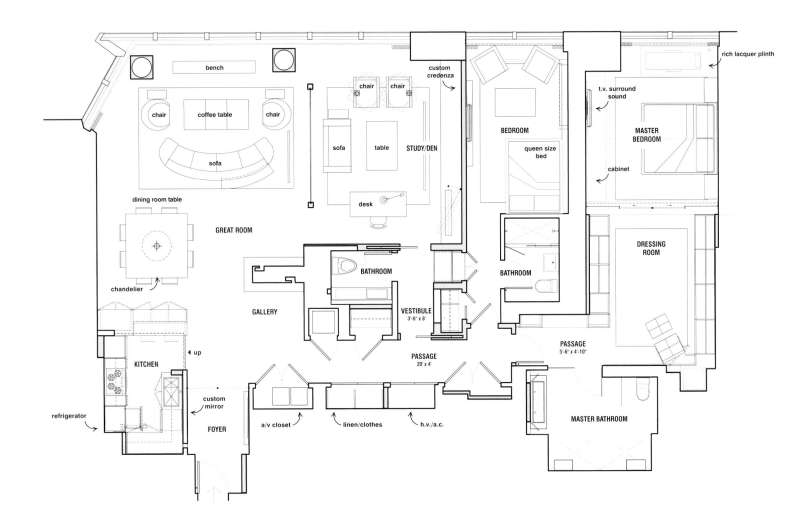

bench

chair | coffee table | chair

sofa

chair | chair

custom credenza

sofa | table | STUDY/DEN

BEDROOM

rich lacquer plinth

t.v. surround sound

MASTER BEDROOM

dining room table

GREAT ROOM

desk

queen size bed

cabinet

chandelier

BATHROOM

DRESSING ROOM

BATHROOM

GALLERY

VESTIBULE
3'-6" x 8'

up

PASSAGE
5'-6" x 4'-10"

KITCHEN

PASSAGE
20' x 4'

refrigerator

custom mirror

FOYER

a/v closet

linen/clothes

h.v./a.c.

MASTER BATHROOM

Opposite: Delicate stiletto-legged furnishings anchor the elegance while keeping the peace of the place. The clear glass table was designed by J. Robert Scott, and 1950s Italian modernist chairs are by Paola Buffa. **Following pages:** A freestanding glass panel framed in black absolute stone separates the living room from the study and media lounge. Wood shelving with a stone surface hides the audio-visual equipment. The press of a button raises the television into view.

Above: The master bedroom suite is silenced with seamless glass pocket-door sliders. Blinds lower automatically so the owners can move freely through the dressing room, complete with his-and-her closets. A chaise lounge provides meditative city views. The leather bed is from Poltrona Frau; nightstands are from Cappellini.

Above: The guest bedroom parallels the master bedroom's understated style. Its soft palette invites relaxation. Twin reading chairs from Cassina can swivel to the view.

Following pages: The master bath is wrapped in marble and detailed with white glass tiles; the blue onyx sink is steps from the ten-foot-long, his-and-her shower.

No one can deny Jennifer is purposed. Her goals are clear. Predictable places must be transformed into ethereal escapes. Views that should be captured are. Light that can come in does. Confined spaces unfold like the giant bloom of a dahlia.

A hedge-fund manager and his fashion designer wife hired Jennifer for the redo of their 3,500-square-foot Upper East Side condo. What was interesting was that the 2001 ultramodern high rise, the creation of Robert A. M. Stern, told two different architectural stories. Outside modern; inside, a plethora of classic details, small rooms, and low ceilings. These would be plucked like weeds to make room for Jennifer's architectural garden of delight, a place soon to be defined as elegant and modern with classical tones. A total gut was soon on the clock. A new layout came with the territory.

It was, as Jennifer explains, an axis that moved from the kitchen in the east, to the living room in the west, to the library in the south. Windows punctuated end points framing the stunning city views. And, for an unexpected design twist, Jennifer designed and built a library that also functioned as the entry gallery. The books' colorful spines introduce color and texture to a room that is full of pure, clean space.

Opposite: The classic Post spine: a pristine pathway of matte limestone, wrapped in ultra-white lacquered walls, and rooms mapped left, right, and ahead. Light insets are low to the floor, providing candlelight-quality guides when dusk falls. Frosted glass sliders close off private areas and allow daylight to filter into the space.

Above: The hall is an oasis of calm. **Previous pages:** Apple-green draperies frame the living room views, and boxed grasses connect nature to this high-rise perch. Low, wide furnishings from Cassina float on slender metal posts, emphasizing all things light and elegant. **Opposite:** Black leather chairs contain the dining area.

Following pages: The sleek, ultramodern kitchen is infused with natural light coming off the spine. When we think kitchen and hearth, we think clean and efficient, and the stainless steel backsplash and countertops bring that concept to the forefront. Cabinetry from Poggen Pohl keeps the space crisp and absent of visual noise.

Jennifer has a few unbreakable design rules. High on the list—and what is perhaps the very essence of her work—is elegance that is always both fluid and serene. To accomplish these dreamy, spa-like rooms takes a razor-like focus and relentless attention to detail, from marrying the veining of marble flooring to determining the shape of drawer pulls. Everything has a purpose; everything is rooted from a plan.

This California project came to Jennifer as so many do. Her client, a well-known performer, saw an example of her work—a take-your-breath-away apartment with views of Central Park—and wanted the look duplicated here. But there was little common ground to transport the concept.

There were many curves here—a no-no if Post's work is to bloom properly. The space had to be completely reworked, which she did in her sketchpad in one day, furiously drawing out a new plan on site.

The house's seemingly endless views of distant valleys and undulating mountain ranges would ultimately drive everything—from furniture choices, to fabric, to the elimination of walls that would surface new views from within the space.

Jennifer partnered as the interior architect with architects William Hablinski and Brian Wesley Biglin. Walls came down, ceilings were heightened three feet to max out at twelve, and walls of glass opened interior rooms. Her signature layout of a gallery, or spine as she calls it, running the length of the house with all rooms branching off, suited the site perfectly and maximized the views and light.

Inspired by the natural topography, she created a fitting outdoor setting with the addition of a reflecting pool, a fountain, and an infinity pool. These ribbons of blue that surround the home keep the peace and stave off the din of daily life. It is hard to imagine the jangle of a cell phone or the clang of a printer interrupting what she has accomplished.

White walls and marble floors provide the painterly landscape with a fitting frame, and Jennifer's choices of soft, natural fabrics, buttery leathers, and a rich stew of woods—from ebony to sycamore and ash—infuse the space with distinct textures, supporting her overall theme. Furnishings are sleek and comfortable, and as always chosen to keep views open and emphasize ceiling height. Chairs and tables all share a pleasing sculptural quality.

"Furnishings are not just places to sit," says Jennifer. "They are pieces of art in a room—structures with beautiful shapes that work with the surfaces they stand on and the palette that surrounds. They can be metaphors for the setting and ultimately the poetry of a place."

Opposite: Twin antique benches found by Jennifer add artistic, architectural punctuation points to the formal front foyer in the main gallery, with views of the living room.

Preceding pages: The arched ceiling and pointed cutout of glass telescope to the fountain and landscaped backyard. White leather furnishings by J. Robert Scott in the sleek seating area make a design statement. The white marble floor creates a stunning pathway around the chocolate rug by Odegard to the patio beyond.

Above: Stepping into the master bath, wrapped in pale sea-green glass tiles and mirror, is like floating into a dreamy sea cave. The marble floor tiles recall stones polished by swirling tidal waters. **Opposite:** Twelve-foot ceilings hold sheers from Robert Allen that can transform the mood within this pristine cluster of seating.

Preceding pages: The dining room appears as if a portion of the outdoors has been replicated in the form of fabric and furnishings. The moss-green rug from Hokanson Carpet resembles a grassy knoll planted with a forest of chairs. The J. Robert Scott table leads our gaze to the wall of glass, making an effortless transition to nature.

Opposite and above: A French limestone foyer sets the stage. "You have just enough information at that point so that expectations are set for what will soon unfold," says Jennifer. "It entices. You hopefully want more." **Following pages:** Views reach from the reflecting pool past emerald-green plantings to the starry sky beyond.

Here was an architectural journey with Jennifer, the perfect guide: seven thousand square feet of raw real estate in a landmark Tribeca building. The challenge, or for her, an invigorating design mission, was to work *only* with dark brown and cream, the lady of the house's preferred palette. Not a problem for Jennifer. When she is not working strictly in white, her palette easily shifts into more earthy tones.

Post worked in cooperation with New York architect Steven Learner on the space, which comprised the seventh and eighth floors of the building, plus a magnificent rooftop terrace. It was a perfect coupling as both are equally adept at analyzing spaces at the micro level and then ultimately assigning a purpose for every detail.

The home is now a blend of classic and modern—a calculated, balanced synergy of shapes, color, material, and light. Dark-stained wood floors, rich brown wood furnishings, and cream-colored limestone establish the palette. Jennifer also utilized several of her signature design elements: extra-wide halls, few doors, and a magnificent double-height transparent staircase that gently unfolds to the lower floor.

Opposite and following pages: What was once white oak are now stunning ebonized panels framing the limestone-bordered fireplace in the living room. Custom-designed couches and chairs sit atop a thick rug from Odegard. Comfort is a sub-theme in this home, with children and (if you can imagine) two Golden Retrievers.

Above: The contrasting chocolate and white palette extends into the contemporary kitchen. Beautiful backless stools invite guests to perch while dinner is being plated.

Above: A nine-by-three-foot opening in the dining room ceiling brings in natural light from the family room above, and, as Post says, adds an unexpected dose of drama.

Above: The cascading staircase seems more archeological in its posture as the backbone of the space. The open stairs offer views supreme from all directions.

Above: The kitchen is tucked off the main spine of the floor. Its wide opening facilitates moving in and out, as well as carrying on conversations with those passing by.

Above: In the family room, seating circles the fireplace, and with furnishings atop a wood-toned rug by Odegard, the room is both casual and warm. **Opposite:** Floor-to-ceiling limestone wraps the master bathroom, and a massive skylight provides a window to the world of jets passing, stars twinkling, sunrises, and sunsets.

Following pages: The master bedroom, a blend of caramel, white, and brown, is a Zen-like composition of rounded edges and soft fabrics. Gauze-like window treatments screen the sunlight and provide soft illumination. The Ultrasuede bed by Rudin is from Robert Allen. On the wall is a photograph from the owner's collection.

The old 1860s sewing needle factory turned loft space, with fabulous views of the Empire State Building, was a welcome project for Jennifer. She had designed another city loft for this client back in the 1990s, so he knew her style, and she knew his. But the goal for the finance executive this time was to turn an entire floor of raw loft space into more of a home, with clearly delineated rooms. Jennifer saw the potential in this 5,300-square-foot space, with its row of support columns, twelve-foot ceilings, and twenty-four massive windows encircling the perimeter.

Her final design did not abandon the open, fluid movement that defines lofts (and her work for that matter). She used the generous proportions to her advantage and worked with an L shape consisting of two one-hundred-foot legs that ultimately made for space washed in light and filled with views. It was also the perfect plan for segregating public and private spaces.

The shorter leg of the L, the master bath/dressing room, is the ultimate decompression zone for the busy bachelor. It is equipped with both a walk-in shower and a whirlpool bath. Storage closets line the space and lead to a dressing room. The second leg, the public space, is open and inviting. At twice the width of the suite, it includes the entrance hall, living area, dining area, kitchen, media room, gym, two guest bedrooms and baths, and a library/office.

"Even if he works all night on his computer, he has to eventually get to the bedroom. With this layout he would get to stroll through all eight rooms, past his art collection, and all twenty-four of the huge windows that wrap the space. He'd catch those great views of the Empire State Building and the rooflines jutting into the sky—and maybe, just maybe, he'd catch his breath, for just a second," Jennifer says.

Opposite: With low seating and twelve-foot ceilings, the living room feels exceptionally spacious. A Jacqueline Humphries painting provides a pleasing wash of color on the neutral wall. **Following pages:** The space is bathed in light. Clustered seating invites conversation. Two steel drum tables from Dennis Miller continue the circle.

Above: From the cool, crisp limestone entry, floating before the sea of cherry wood pathways, visitors can pause, take in the light and views, and breathe easy.

Above: The pure white wall accentuates the richness and warmth of the Brazilian walkways. Rich Brazilian cherry built-ins line the walls of the hallway to the master suite.

Above: The twelve-foot columns, architectural bookmarks to the past, provide a natural guide deep into the space. It is ironic that what once perhaps bore sweat and noise is now a serene place that radiates calm. **Previous pages:** The ingenious symmetry extends from seating to console to dining space and beyond to the kitchen.

Above: The master bath has Brazilian cherry built-ins with blue slate countertops. A deep chocolate ribbon of tile is inset into the velvety limestone that wraps the space. **Following pages:** Contemporary art adds spikes of energy and color to the walls. The rug is from Patterson, Flynn & Martin; the console is from Pierce Martin.

Think Jennifer Post and now think yoga; think energy worker. Her work seems to have a slow-building calm, a rush tide of openness that gets higher and higher. Step into her spaces and you are present, in the moment, and you will breathe deeply. And like a good yoga master, she takes down the stifling knots and opens the channels of both interior and exterior spaces.

Jennifer cross-pollinates the fundamental lessons of yoga into her clients' homes. After all, as she has so often declared, the walls that surround and hold us serve a much higher purpose. Our homes offer privacy, a safe haven, and a solitary island to rejuvenate our spirits.

Living in the city, while wonderful and rich, can be overstimulating to the senses. Crisscrossing noisy streets, running to elevators, maneuvering narrow corridors to meetings—then home to a maze of small rooms, with too many doors. Are we breathing deeply? Are we present? Not so much.

Now, fast forward to this 3,200-square-foot apartment and the couple's desire to go comfortable and modern, to elevate its purpose. The layout that stopped the life flow and fluidity of the place was the first thing to be readjusted. Think of walls as blocking energy. Remove them, and energy begins to move; views open; light comes. The clients now live in a space that breathes, flows unencumbered, and offers calmness. In the hours spent there, whether two or twenty-four, rejuvenation of the mind and spirit will ultimately follow.

Opposite: In this sea-of-white living room Jennifer introduced the warmest of hues, conjuring thoughts of a summer sunrise when the sky is streaked in burnt orange swathes, and the color bands shift and stretch with the wind. Red leather cubes are from Hermès. Hugues Chevalier chairs invite conversation. The ottoman is by Studium V.

Previous pages: Area rugs in pale hues float above the velvet-soft limestone floors, demarcating rooms. A single sculpture distinguishes the seating area—the shape, suggestive of intimacy and coming together, is a perfect metaphor for this peaceful gathering place. The space flows freely into a light-filled dining room.

Opposite: We peek here into the study. A leggy sculptural desk with a transparent glass top keeps the mood light, the space crisp. A pad of golden rug adds warmth underfoot and provides a splash of color. **Above:** The bronze sculpture, *Expecting* by Dimitry German—a favorite of Jennifer's—suggests wings, flight, and freedom.

Above: Our imagination is captured in the foyer by this unusual clay and bronze Hanneke Beaumont sculpture of a man sitting, perhaps contemplating the views.
Opposite: A ceramic bubble pot by Abigail Simpson sits adjacent to a sculptural chair in the kitchen. Light and shapes merge, providing a fitting backdrop for the art.

Following pages: With the palest of lemon walls and shades of amber accents, the master bedroom is elegant and relaxed. A whimsical 1940s James Mont chair was mined at Liz O'Brien's New York gallery. A sand-colored Einstein Moomjy rug is a cozy touchdown. The bed and dresser are from Format; coverlets are by Frette.

Jennifer's concept for the Boys and Girls Club Decorator's Show House was to create a space that instantly transports us from the city to an exotic, opulent lounge and spa. She re-created that moment—when we first open the door to a coveted piece of paradise in a faraway dreamy resort—of instant decompression, the deep breath that says you've arrived. What is missing here in white sand and ocean is made up for in the magnificent treetop views of Central Park.

"The idea was to have this wonderful, private escape where you could walk off the elevator and close off the stress of the day," says Jennifer.

The landmark brownstone with ample space, including a walkout terrace, was the perfect design canvas from which to work. But prior to the buildout and design of the interior, some demolition was required to take down walls and open the space room to room. New ceilings were designed for the living room, and crown moldings were extracted to further streamline the look.

Jennifer's color palette was simple and classic, with muted tones, ebony, and white. Dark espresso-brown wood floors with a high sheen presented the ideal grounding for the sleek, sculptural furnishings. Priceless African and Asian art, artifacts, and design accents are seeded throughout the space, providing a profound juxtaposition of ultra-contemporary and tribal cultures within these walls.

The space includes a cozy, comfortable living room, and massage and yoga areas. Jennifer opted to carpet the terrace, covering cold, hard surface pavers to make this area an extension of the interior space and maintain the cozy, quiet factor.

Soft, plush fabrics like cashmere and cotton chenille support the casual, comfortable theme of the space. A true testament to the success of the design came when the house was purchased and the new owners decided that Jennifer's fantasy escape would now be theirs.

Opposite: Twin massage tables are separated by a sleek mahogany console that holds towels and massage oils. **Following pages:** In front of the massage tables Jennifer raised the floor for yoga practice. Sheer curtains let light play and keep the spa mood. The walls are adorned by photos of African tribe members and sculpture.

Above: A bronze jaguar bench sculpture by Judy McKensey stands on all fours as if gazing at the tribal mask on the living room wall. A glowing sconce recalls the heat of a jungle's midday sun. Furnishings sit atop a plush rug from Patterson, Flynn & Martin. Jennifer designed the walnut entertainment center to the right.

Above: Chairs are covered in cotton chenille, and black cashmere cocoons the low couch, custom designed by Jennifer. We see here how open the room-to-room access is: from the living room lounge into the massage room, and off to the terrace. **Following pages:** The terrace, edged in boxwoods, retains privacy and peace.

At dusk, when the interior lights glow against the snow on this nine-thousand-foot-high Aspen mountaintop, this vacation home's chiseled frame—open to the outside in a rhythmic cut of windows—recalls the snowflakes that surround.

And just as no two snowflakes are alike, this getaway is unique in its total design form and from room to room. That was the goal for Jennifer here, as well as to honor the grand views of blue sky and woods.

She characterizes this ski-in, ski-out home as a modern version of post and beam. Rich mahogany floors, stone fireplaces, Caesarstone countertops in the kitchen, and subdued earth tones all dovetail with the natural landscape. A diversion for the designer from her signature snow-white walls to a vanilla tone came as a result of her desire to reflect the warmer exterior tones.

The layout was intended to distinguish the public rooms with furniture placement rather than walls, encouraging the family to gather together. The kitchen is open to the living room, dining room, and children's lounge. Fabrics and furnishings are casual, sturdy, and fuss-free.

Opposite: This long view of the downstairs spaces emphasizes the unique design of this house. Gray mohair and white chenille furnishings are comfortable and understated. The pale-sand-and-brown-hued stones of the fireplace create a dramatic hearth and focal point. Its simplicity gives center stage to the four seasons of colorful views.

Above: It was important, Jennifer says, to create a beautiful foyer. A mirror framed in bronze reflects the steel staircase with mahogany treads. The birch bench was custom made by Brooklyn artist Eric Slayton. **Previous pages:** The children's lounge palette echoes the living room with couches in Jennifer's custom wool-blended corduroy.

Above: The two-storied wall of glass and stone presented an opportunity for a bit of haiku sculptural poetry. Jennifer commissioned this textural trio of sculptures.
Following pages: Different ceiling heights, rectangles of windows, the weave of the staircase, and the twinkle of recessed lights come together to form a perfect whole.

SKI ROOM

DINING ROOM
10' x 8'

FAMILY ROOM
11'-6" x 14'-1"

coffee table

FIRE PIT

STORAGE

MECHANICAL

LIVING ROOM
15'-6" x 15'

fire place

OUTDOOR DINING ROOM

HOT TUB

GARAGE

KITCHEN

ENTRY/
LOUNGE

BATHROOM

GUEST/KIDS
BEDROOM

GUEST BEDROOM
SUITE
18'-10" x 12'-7"

light fixture
above

GUEST BATHROOM

Opposite, above: Rich chocolate-wood cabinetry—designed by Jennifer and capped in glacier-white Caesarstone—creates a balance of casual and elegant. **Below:** The tub evokes a giant pebble, made shiny smooth from being tossed on a local riverbed. The velvet-smooth Colorado River limestone flooring carries the analogy further, and the wood hues reflect the diversity of the trees outside. **Following pages:** At dusk this family getaway glows like a hearth atop one of Aspen's highest mountains.

When Jennifer designed this couple's mountaintop retreat in Aspen, she succeeded at making the ski-in, ski-out house a pleasing balance of casual and elegant, never once tipping the scale. But here, at their year-round home in Scarsdale, New York, they wanted a more pristine, tailored look. They admired the house Jennifer designed in Beverly Hills (see page 224) and how it seems to so beautifully silence the day.

Today, a gracious foyer leads to the formal living room to the left and dining room to the right. A lounge, where the family watches television, sits at the very end of the home off the living room. The public rooms, in Jennifer's words, are all about being seductive. Accomplishing her goal are a color palette of black and smoky gray; silk and cashmere fabrics; and high-gloss ebony floors. The only curves that catch our eye are the rounded arches between rooms, and the larger-than-life sculptures that stand like sensual exclamation points within the space.

The gorgeous leaded-glass windows provide an elegant framing to the views. The square-on-square panes are in visual harmony with the ninety-degree angles of the contemporary furnishings.

Playful, warm, and cool colors come into the private areas: the family lounge, the office, and the children's bedrooms and playroom.

Opposite and following pages: The long living room called for a unique seating arrangement. Coupled black alpaca loveseats encourage conversation, and the Nepalese silk rug is cozy and luxurious. Twin coffee tables from J. Robert Scott are finished in a matte lacquer. Post-designed bronze end tables have leather inserts.

Above: The black-framed, glass-topped table from J. Robert Scott, surrounded by eight black Catherine Memmi leather chairs, is enhanced by sheer black drapes and a seductive sculpture by Kevin Kelly. **Previous pages:** Buttery soft Lazzoni couches can accommodate guest spillover from the living room or provide a quiet hideaway.

Above: An outdoor patio functions as an extension of the rooms within. Plantings and furnishings designate separate outdoor spaces for dining and relaxing. Narrow, elongated sand-colored stone pavers carpet the floor underfoot. Plantings provide the textures and variegated color spectrum of a delightful, calming garden.

Above: The Tudor-style windows bathe the contemporary-styled workspace in light and views. The dining table and chairs align with the crisp kitchen cabinetry.

Opposite: The plush couches are ideal for watching television. A white silk rug introduces texture. An oversized hassock with surface inserts doubles as a server.

Following pages: The entrance foyer is sculptural and fluid, with high-gloss ebony floors. The wood banister, rooted in fine stainless-steel posts, keeps the climb open and anchored in modern. Custom concrete sculptures by Eric Slayton, a New York–based sculptor and furniture maker, support the tailored, refined design.

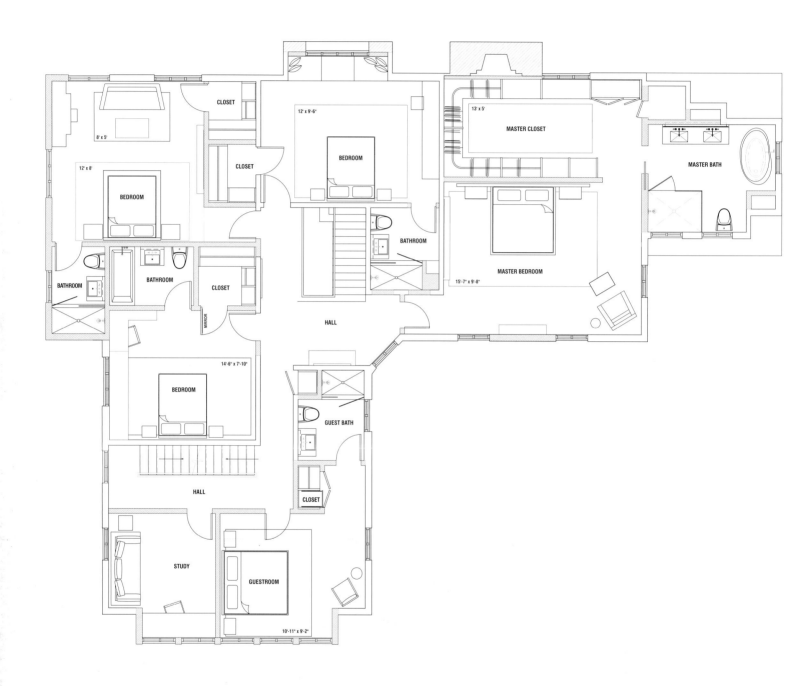

CLOSET

8' x 5'

12' x 8'

BEDROOM

BATHROOM

BATHROOM

CLOSET

12' x 9'-6"

BEDROOM

CLOSET

MIRROR

HALL

14'-6" x 7'-10"

BEDROOM

BATHROOM

HALL

GUEST BATH

CLOSET

STUDY

GUESTROOM

10'-11" x 9'-2"

MASTER CLOSET

13' x 5'

MASTER BATH

MASTER BEDROOM

15'-7" x 9'-8"

Opposite: Steps from the bedroom, the spa-like master bath is minimalist to the max. **Following pages:** Jennifer's furnishings make two fluid paths in perfect symmetry, leading to the outside hearth, where conversation can continue into the night. One can almost hear the glasses clinking to a toast. **Pages 134–35:** Here we see the Tudor in all it grandness, a beautifully preserved manor serving as the wrapping for the new design era that has germinated within its stucco walls.

It took the purchase of two apartments, one on top of the other, to achieve the clients' goal of capturing the world-class views of Manhattan's Central Park, Hayden Planetarium, and Museum of Natural History, framed in the windows of their home.

But the coveted apartment in this prewar building was full of crown moldings and other period architectural details that weighed down the five thousand square feet of space. It was as far away from a Post design as anything could be, and, no surprise, it all had to go.

"The objective was to create a voluminous space, and key to that was to take these two 2,500-square-foot spaces back to the studs and start from scratch.

"My first thought when I met with the clients in the space was that this needs a wow factor, as well as light and pathways that would increase and accentuate the articulation of space."

It took four schematic designs to achieve their shared vision. Big, light-inhibiting walls came down; glass walls or sliders went up. Two one-hundred-foot hallways run the entire length of the home, each at Jennifer's standard view-opening fifty-inch width. Doors disappeared to welcome movement in and out of rooms and bring in maximum washes of natural light.

A major architectural focal point was the magnificent, airy, floating staircase built to join the floors. No solid wall obstructs the view from the staircase to the sixteenth floor, nor to the bottom of the fifteenth. Instead seamless glass walls appear on landings, floor to floor, for full views.

The top floor, the more public area, is comprised of a large kitchen, family room, children's playroom, study, living room, and dining room, as well as a custom-built bar. The lower level includes a grownups' lounge complete with an audio/video entertainment center and a couch that can comfortably seat up to twelve. In addition are the master bedroom suite, three other bedrooms, and laundry and storage facilities.

Opposite: A striking work by Jason Martin gives us pause on the landing of this five-thousand-square-foot apartment in a prewar building on New York's Upper West Side. The wide limestone hall, cool and organic, guides us through the space, with a playful punch of sculpted orange framing a distant view of his-and-her offices.

Previous pages: A black slate wall is a dramatic focal point in this white room with accents in midnight black. The custom-made silk rug from Nepal sits atop the limestone slabs, a fitting surface for a cluster of Italian-made furniture. Rooftop views rise up the windows, creating architectural stalagmites to capture our gaze.

Above: Lemon-yellow couches on a stain-resistant rug of the same hue distinguish the children's playroom, which is tucked off a main hall not far from the kitchen.
Opposite: Floor-to-ceiling glass pocket doors open to hallways and separate the rooms from one another, while keeping light moving freely through the space.

Above: With the kitchen and breakfast area as one space, light and rooftop views are enjoyed by both the cook and the guests who dine here. White cabinetry sits back in the roomscape. Chairs by Moura Starr and a Cappellini table add harmonious shapes. An abstract on the wall is as good as a strong cappuccino to wake you.

Above: When you sit on the opposite side of the table, the news of the day is before you on a thoughtfully placed flat-screen television flush with the wall. The wall partition keeps the flow going in two paths for easy exit to other rooms. A golden yellow rug by Patterson, Flynn & Martin insures quiet and adds warmth underfoot.

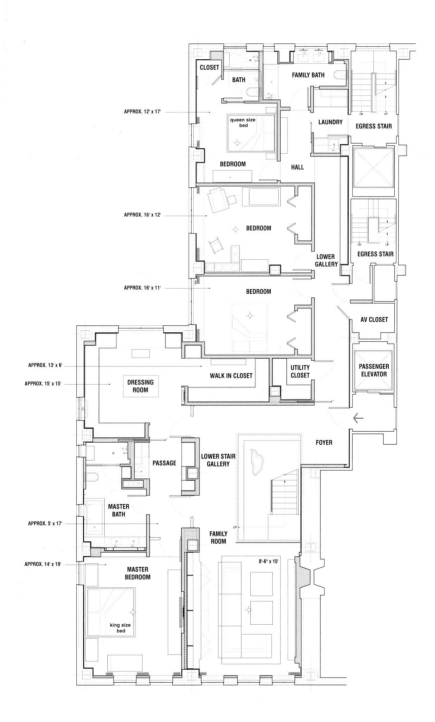

CLOSET

BATH

FAMILY BATH

APPROX. 12' x 17'

queen size
bed

LAUNDRY

EGRESS STAIR

BEDROOM

HALL

APPROX. 16' x 12'

BEDROOM

LOWER
GALLERY

EGRESS STAIR

APPROX. 16' x 11'

BEDROOM

AV CLOSET

APPROX. 13' x 6'

WALK IN CLOSET

UTILITY
CLOSET

PASSENGER
ELEVATOR

APPROX. 15' x 15'

DRESSING
ROOM

FOYER

PASSAGE

LOWER STAIR
GALLERY

MASTER
BATH

APPROX. 5' x 17'

FAMILY
ROOM

APPROX. 14' x 19'

MASTER
BEDROOM

8'-6" x 15'

king size
bed

Opposite: Beneath the living room we look into the glass-framed family room. As one descends the limestone-capped stairs the views unfold for a sense of openness.

Above: Step into the master bath and leave the city din in another time zone. Every design detail was meticulously tailored to the space by Jennifer. It is easy to imagine yourself floating through the space, moving from one task area to another, with no disruptive sounds, just the soothing, rhythmic splashing of water to stone.

Above: A glass-walled shower, wrapped floor to ceiling in a tile pattern, recalls the rhythm of falling raindrops. The oversized showerhead promises to fulfill the concept. Again we see how effectively the designer can work the less-is-more mantra into the corners of a home, never compromising to add a detail without a purpose.

Above: The dressing room was designed for freedom of movement while artfully maintaining space for storage. **Opposite:** The original 1970s Sputnik chandelier infuses the master bedroom with a twinkle, day or night. Linens in a brushstroke of blue, something between a Caribbean sea and sky, play off the art by Sarah Morris.

Following pages: A two-story abstract painting by Sarah Morris recalls the colorful precision cuts of stained glass, brightening and energizing the climb up or down the glass and steel stairway. The thread of orange as an accent color culminates on the back wall of the lower level with two whimsical paintings by Julian Opie.

It is hard to imagine a more perfect commission. Magazine articles that had sung the praises of Jennifer brought this client calling. No need for a presentation of her work, no time lag on a decision to move forward. One meeting and the only directive was, do what you do. It was as simple and clean as her portfolio. And that brought a rogue wave of creativity to this five-thousand-square-foot Miami penthouse.

Soon this frenetic business giant would have a place where sky and gentle tides would fill the view and clock the day across expanses of space. Building out transparent rooms, Jennifer used glass to catch light on natural curves and capture views from every turn: the beach below and distant views of the city, rooflines breaking into the blue like the tops of sandcastles.

The rooms move freely into one another from wide, view-capturing framed openings, and high ceilings lift the airy space skyward. No extraneous design details here. White lacquered walls, custom furnishings, marble flooring, and a palette of ocean blues create a sea of calm.

Opposite: Polished stone flooring makes for a heavenly path to the eleven-foot-tall glass doors that welcome us to the space. The curl of the sculpture gently guides us in, the distant view impossible to resist. Step in and we are swallowed in light. A Great Dane named Zeek, a magnificent sculpture himself, gives us perspective.

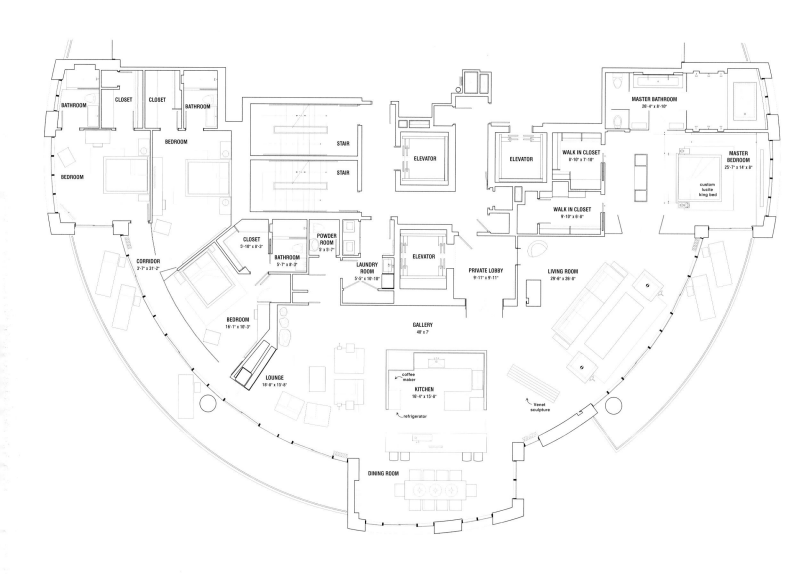

BATHROOM CLOSET CLOSET BATHROOM

BEDROOM

MASTER BATHROOM
26'-4" x 8'-10"

BEDROOM

STAIR

ELEVATOR

ELEVATOR

WALK IN CLOSET
8'-10" x 7'-10"

MASTER
BEDROOM
25'-7" x 14' 8"

STAIR

custom
lucite
king bed

WALK IN CLOSET
9'-10" x 6'-8"

CORRIDOR
3'-7" x 31'-2"

CLOSET
5'-10" x 8'-3"

POWDER
ROOM
5' x 5'-7"

BATHROOM
5'-7" x 8'-3"

ELEVATOR

LAUNDRY
ROOM
5'-5" x 10'-10"

PRIVATE LOBBY
9'-11" x 9'-11"

LIVING ROOM
29'-6" x 26'-8"

BEDROOM
16'-1" x 10'-3"

GALLERY
40' x 7'

coffee
maker

LOUNGE
18'-8" x 15'-8"

KITCHEN
16'-4" x 15'-8"

Venet
sculpture

refrigerator

DINING ROOM

Opposite: A thirteen-foot custom couch and eleven-foot coffee table sit atop a custom silk rug in the same turquoise-green found in the veins of an abalone shell.
Previous pages: In addition to layering her spaces with light by carving halls, windows, and skylights, Jennifer introduces sculpture—something that connects to the space. The steel sculpture commissioned from Bernar Venet echoes the three-quarter moon of the floor plan, but also suggests the curl of a wave so familiar in the view.

Above: Nothing should distract from this view, so Jennifer custom-designed Lucite furnishings. A driftwood chair called *Dandelion* from Yves Boucard evokes a sea anemone stilled on the ocean floor. **Previous pages:** This bedroom sits on a corridor of glass, keeping it open to the views. Glass goes opaque at the press of a button.

Above: Off the living room is a private sunbathing deck that takes in the vast, unobstructed views of the sand below and the sea ahead. Custom-colored glass panels of lagoon blue keep views in check, even when one is reclining. White lounge chairs and a side table with a tangerine-colored top are from Richard Schultz.

Above: The master bath, a continuation of the marble flooring that weaves through the house, is wrapped in white lacquered walls and ends in a luxurious six-head shower.

Above: A little puff of a chair is shaped like a sea creature. A Lucite table with removable tray top by the Italian designer Micucci allows ample space for cocktails.

Above and opposite: With just a few architectural cues, like the high stools and a work surface, you realize you've stepped over the threshold into the kitchen and then into the dining room. Only a hint to define where you are—no interruption in the flow or in the vistas to the sea ahead. A trio of Schonbek chandeliers links the spaces.

Following pages: The family room is nearly identical in palette to the living room, so rooms in this Miami penthouse seem more like small ocean inlets where views change but the feeling stays the same. Slightly different seating, a bit more casual in shape, distinguishes the space. A shaded patio is accessed through glass sliders.

It was decided that this, the sister residence of the Miami penthouse project, would make the perfect guesthouse in the sky. Just as it is common to create a private, fully functional guesthouse a walk down a pathway from the main house on a luxury estate, these guest quarters are steps down the hallway from the owners. The stunning views are shared, the décor thoughtfully dovetails, and visits to and from come easily.

The building of the two spaces was staggered, but timing aside, the architectural and design theme would ultimately cross-pollinate, linking them in an inspired spirit of oneness. White on white continues as a theme, but here Jennifer introduced touches of lemon yellow to the ultraclean, edited design mix. While spare and tailored, it is, in its softness, inviting, cozy, and like all of Post's work, calm. What distinguishes this space is its smaller scale and more relaxed style.

In discussions with Jennifer, the owner noted that he wanted to use this space, as well, when guests were not in town. He would come to the space to practice yoga—so this would be a little getaway within a getaway. Jennifer happily complied and designed a yoga studio within the seven rooms. The architectural marriage of dual purposes in this glass hideaway came without a hitch. It was a pleasurable high note in the design process since the designer herself begins her days with yoga sessions. She knew precisely how to make it flow.

Opposite: White lacquered walls and Thassos marble flooring, empty of distraction, emphasize that less truly is more. **Following pages:** Seating is clustered around the view. The white lacquer coffee table, with flamingo sculptures from Christine Bell Antiques, seems to float on the water view; a sliver-of-a-moon-shaped lounge beckons.

CLOSET

BATHROOM

BEDROOM

WALK IN CLOSET

yoga
sculpture

Kamp artwork

LOUNGE

t.v. w/surround sound

MASTER
BATHROOM

PASSAGE

EAST BALCONY

integral side tables

LOUNGE

GALLERY

DINING ROOM

WEST
BALCONY

custom
queen bed

KITCHEN

LIVING ROOM

t.v. w/surround sound

13' x 9'-11"

t.v.

BATHROOM

CLOSET

STORAGE ROOM

LAUNDRY ROOM

PRIVATE LOBBY

POWDER
ROOM

BATHROOM

STAIR

ELEVATOR

ELEVATOR

STAIR

ELEVATOR

Opposite and following pages: Views of the family room show how the space unfolds—first into the kitchen and then into the bedroom. We see firsthand how Jennifer has created open vistas in the space with high ceilings, wide walkways, and restrained design details. The Ligne Roset sofa and chairs, organic and round-edged, bloom with golden yellow pillows that recall sea sponges. It is easy to imagine how the tiny ceiling lights give a starry night feeling here as the day unwinds.

Above and opposite: As if a giant White Admiral butterfly flitted through, leaving powdery traces of earth-bound colors behind, one bedroom has touches of blue, another has flecks of mango, and a third has dashes of tangerine. These views beautifully isolate the drama and serenity that come with Jennifer's numbered furnishings.

Following pages: The beautiful bronze sculpture of a figure in child's pose called *La Priere* by Jean Lambert-Rucki designates this room for yoga. The energy that moves through the body in practice seems echoed in a Thilo Heinzman mixed-media work on the wall. A Patterson, Flynn & Martin sisal carpet takes au natural to a new posture.

MIAMI BEACH ROOFTOP COLORS WASH A ROOFTOP RETREAT

And so, the architectural and design story continues, and climbs to the rooftop, where Miami's blue sky meets the water, and soft breezes and powdery sands break from the luxurious glass escape below. Here, Jennifer's clients and their guests can feel the heat of day and drink in the ever-changing light. This playground in the sky is where Jennifer declares her fusion of color. The shades of blue and fresh, zesty orange—which sequined the main house and guest quarters via fabric and glass—now merge in paint, fabric, and furnishings. But here the palette is completed in sky, making the perfect marriage of colors.

Jennifer worked the rooftop space as she normally would (but this time, high ceilings were already in place). For her client, there are four bays for entertaining (including a full kitchen), relaxing (there is even a freestanding shower), and exercising (in an open-air yoga studio).

She designed and built a twenty-foot-high wall to clearly distinguish the sections of these concrete rooms, carrying the deep tangerine hue through in fabric, furnishings, decorative rock paths, towels, yoga mats, and paint. A cool-to-the-touch, pebble-textured floor, concrete banquettes, and open-air views framed in rectangles of steel and concrete remain true to the rooftop as an architectural subset.

Opposite: Light and shadows play off the relaxed curve in the tangerine wall, as well as in columns and girders. In the wall's big, angled swing, we are invited to move about and explore. **Following pages:** The thirteen-foot-long banquette is topped by cushions covered in Perennials fabric, their forms crisply outlined in more tangerine.

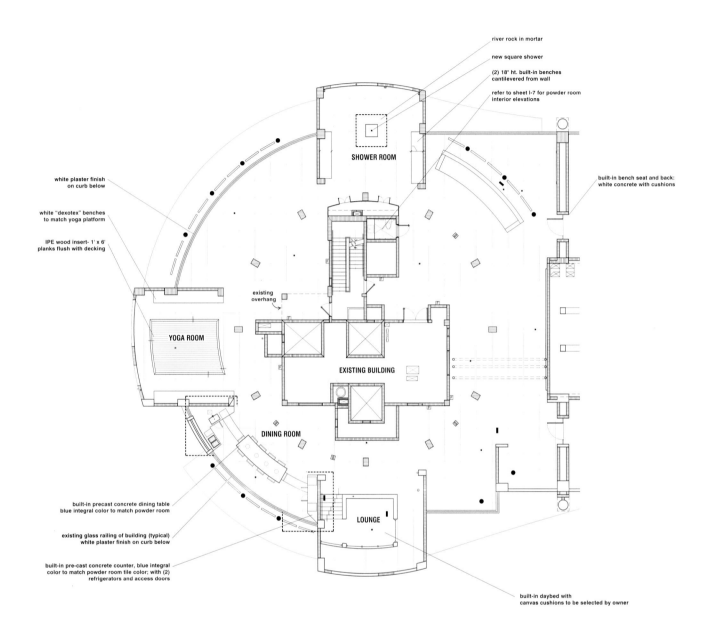

river rock in mortar

new square shower

(2) 18" ht. built-in benches
cantilevered from wall

refer to sheet I-7 for powder room
interior elevations

SHOWER ROOM

built-in bench seat and back:
white concrete with cushions

white plaster finish
on curb below

white "dexotex" benches
to match yoga platform

IPE wood insert- 1' x 6'
planks flush with decking

existing
overhang

YOGA ROOM

EXISTING BUILDING

DINING ROOM

LOUNGE

built-in precast concrete dining table
blue integral color to match powder room

existing glass railing of building (typical)
white plaster finish on curb below

built-in pre-cast concrete counter, blue integral
color to match powder room tile color; with (2)
refrigerators and access doors

built-in daybed with
canvas cushions to be selected by owner

Opposite: Richard Schultz chairs surrounding a white poured-concrete table suggest the posture of a delicate sixteen-legged sea creature that paddled its way to the surface to bask in the Florida sun. **Following pages:** The yoga studio has window cutouts at eye level so the views enhance the sessions. So easy to breathe deeply here, and move through the poses. A wood floor designates the area for mats. **Pages 188–89:** The concrete forms are softened by color, fabric, and the shapes that surround.

There was no need to educate the owners of this home on the supreme benefits of space that is warmed, colored, activated, and even deactivated by natural light. The Virginian couple already lives in a glass house and has for some time. So when Jennifer came on the scene of this nine-hundred-square-foot getaway, clotted with walls obliterating views and boxing up rooms, her design remedy of glass en masse was welcomed.

Her sketchpad delineated a layout that would allow the circa-1960s place to finally breathe. A new architectural heartbeat came, as did a renewed perspective and a fluidity that until now only existed in the elevator ride to the 42nd floor. From each turn of the space are views that tell the story of a Manhattan day: triple smokestacks jutting skyward, plumes spiraling; intricate webs of metal fiber crossing the East River; ferries cutting across the waters.

Amid the calm, white interior are splashes of color from hung art, sculpture, or fabric. Things like laundry and storage, not necessarily in keeping with the rhythm of visual serenity, have been cleverly hidden from view. With a careful balance of objects, art, shapes, form, and color, this is the perfect architectural design recipe for this couple's urban retreat, and a place that continuously feeds their passion for art.

Opposite and following pages: Skim-coated white walls and twenty-four-inch porcelain floor tiles create a virtual playground for light and views. Low, sleek seating guides your eye outward to the city. The hand-tufted rug is from Patterson, Flynn & Martin, and the sculptural painted plywood rocker is by Yves Boucard.

Above: The clean, high-ceilinged entry, with a narrow channel of tiny white pebbles, draws our eye into the space and beyond, to the distant views of river and sky.

Above: The eighteen-foot-long closet disappears behind floor-to-ceiling doors sans hardware. All things that would disturb the visual quiet are completely hidden.

Above: With all rooms open to one another, a functional kitchen with a seamless transition from other rooms was of paramount importance. Jennifer accomplished this by keeping the space snow-white and free of the expected kitchen ornamentation. Tiny door pulls, smooth lacquer finishes, and recessed lighting achieve her goal.

Above: A Zodiaq countertop and backsplash adhered to the plan as well. Here we can look into the kitchen from the dining room. The minimalist design approach succeeds at merging this area into the open-room scheme. For the cook who invites conversation, it is the perfect place to work, chat, and serve at the countertop.

Above and opposite: With white lacquered table and chairs from Poliform, art by LeRone Wilson (aptly titled *Intense White*), and white walls and floors, this slice of the apartment emphasizes the life force that enters from the dramatic window views—the living art that, depending on the time of day, can transform the mood.

Following pages: The bedroom space is defined by the classic Post glass wall. Sheer electronic shades drop down so the owners can ready for a dinner party in privacy. The lacquered platform bed designed by Jennifer resembles a tiny cloud stalled in space. On the far wall, Nathan Slate Joseph's *A Line in the Sand* adds a wakeup call.

APTHORP LETTING THE ARCHITECTURE SPEAK

Here we are invited into the pristine, heavenly, lemon and white work of art that Jennifer calls home. Her 2,500 square feet of elegant, high-ceilinged, uncomplicated, and always spare rooms flow into one another, unencumbered tributaries on an island of calm. Beautiful, tall windows bathe the space in natural light; her pale lemon walls, furnishings, and art appear in a perpetual soft glow.

The space has a whisper-quiet feeling, and we can imagine how this allows a recharging of Post's creative energy at the required lightening speed. Perhaps this was on her mind when she decided to purchase this particular unit at the Apthorp, a grand 1908 landmark building on Manhattan's Upper West Side.

The limestone-clad building, which takes up an entire city block, was conceived by William Waldorf Astor and executed by architects Clinton & Russell. The castle-like entrance, with intricately fashioned wrought-iron gates and a commanding inner courtyard, only hints at the high-detail interiors yet to come.

Having rented other units here, Jennifer had time over the years to imagine this new body of work—how she would strip and paint and bleach and lacquer. How she would update a kitchen, a bath, or a foyer, and happily remain true to the bones of this very special place. Today, the classical architecture she adores is seamlessly dovetailed with her version of modern.

Period architectural details—dark moldings, wainscoting, and mahogany floors—have been completely transformed with the new palette. The contrast is notable. We have escaped *Lohengrin*, Wagner's bleak, dark opera, to the lightness and joy of Vivaldi's *Four Seasons*.

Opposite: It is easy to imagine the dark wood that once wrapped these walls. How the mood has changed. Now, the white and yellow theme not only accentuates the beauty and drama of the architecture, but it draws our eye to all the tiny, distinctive details carved into wood. *Expecting* by Dimitry German punctuates the sea of white.

Previous pages: This telescopic view into Jennifer's high-ceilinged living room is an example of how she marries old-world architecture with modern art forms. From sculptor Barry Flanagan's giant rabbit to the splashes of color in the paintings wrapping the entryway, she sets us up to anticipate what is coming around the corner.

Opposite and above: Jennifer loves the proportions of the rooms: the living room and dining room stretch to sixty feet. The living room windows stand tall, dressed in yards and yards of sheers. Low, sleek Italian furnishings emphasize the high ceilings and spaciousness. The coffee table is by Poltrona Frau; the sofa is by Zanotta.

Above: A simple glass table from Pierce Martin appears in both the kitchen and dining area. **Opposite:** A sisal rug from Patterson, Flynn & Martin delineates the dining area, with a view to a sunny abstract by Catherine Lynch. A European crystal chandelier, a twin of one in the living room, adds a period piece to the modern landscape.

Following pages: Jennifer's bedroom is as dreamy and uncomplicated as a summer cloud. The abstract by Jacqueline Humphries reminds us of the arrival of a new day. Yards of sheers close out the city and keep this a den of peace and relaxation. The low-to-the-floor table is clean, unobtrusive, and perfect for storage.

You may picture Jennifer Post, notebook and pen in hand, clicking across a room in barely there high heels, ready to begin her roughed-out drawings of what could be. Sometimes, however, a hardhat and safety belt are in order, along with the notebook. That was certainly the case when she was called in for a look at the raw space on the sixty-second floor of a West Side high-rise as the building was taking shape. There she was, with winds over Manhattan at her back, working out a layout with steel girders and breathtaking views as her directional guide. Living room here. Master bedroom there. Wide, long gallery there. With light and views maximized, she was able to create a 3,200-square-foot home where life would revolve around the beauty of one of the most famous and coveted views on the planet.

Her clients—the wife, a marketing and sales director for luxury residential properties, and her husband, who runs an asset-management business—gave her free rein. Today, the entry gallery's eight-foot-high oak wall, floating in the space, defines the area but also provides a small tug of anticipation of what is to come. The eight-foot-wide gallery stretches twenty-five feet, with recessed lights at ankle height.

In the living room, dining room, and media room, floor-to-ceiling Italian sliding glass panels function as inside windows, so there are no distractions to stop the eye. Six more panels are planted throughout, fulfilling the same goal and mantra: let there be light.

Furniture and carpets are subtle hues of blue, beige, gray, and olive, allowing the art to take center stage. Works by Ross Bleckner, John Chamberlain, Thomas Ruff, Russell Sharon, Johnny Swing, and Richard Artschwager add color punches throughout this light-filled home.

Opposite: A twenty-five-foot gallery—starry-lit from above and below—is the main spine of the place, where all rooms are rooted. It is a beautiful space that the owners opted to keep clean and totally absent of art and furnishings. The gallery serves as a decompression chamber of sorts that leads to the rest of the home's spaces.

Previous pages: With long, low seating and a view that circles your being, this elegant, sky-bound perch captures the drama of the day's light and passing weather.

216

Above and opposite: Box-lined Holly Hunt chairs covered in suede upholstery, ten-foot-long Holly Hunt leather sofas, and twin coffee tables create a cozy retreat.

Above: An eight-foot-tall oak architectural element provides peeks within the space without closing off the entry gallery. We see the floor-to-ceiling light on either side.

Above: The dining room opens into the media room via glass panels. The custom stained-oak table is surrounded by chairs from Crate & Barrel. Art is by Kara Walker.

Above and opposite: The SieMatic kitchen is as crisp and clean as a tuxedo—tailored, distinct, and elegant. The designer created the look with just a few materials, reaffirming that less is truly more. Counters are Caesarstone, and the floor is limestone. Glass sliders offer views of the New York City skyline from different angles.

Following pages: Jennifer designed a low bench to wrap the periphery of the master bedroom suite. Cloud-gray Ultrasuede covers the low chair and ottoman by Ligne Roset that, with the writing desk, sit atop a Patterson, Flynn & Martin wool rug. Walls are lacquered in four shades of a blue gray, adding dimension.

Here was a commission of monumental proportions. The project goal was to take this sprawling, classic, 12,000-square-foot Georgian Tudor home in Beverly Hills (home to a much-followed celebrity), and give it Post style to the max—inside and out. Today, the stucco exterior and period style remain intact, for the most part, in the front. However, the courtyard, grounds, and interior comprise a one-man resort. The client "wanted this to feel like all the places he had been in the Caribbean," says Jennifer.

Down to the studs went Jennifer and her crew. The floor plan was totally readjusted on both the first and second floors. The narrow 1960s-style hall that connected the four bedrooms on the upper floor—gone. Crown moldings, baseboards, and dark mahogany floors were removed to make way for a clean, white, elegant aesthetic. The tiny windows that made up the back of the house became floor-to-ceiling glass walls, windows, and ten-foot-wide glass sliders that looked out to what would become the new loggia and terrace.

And down came the traditional staircase, dark, thick, and woody. Jennifer deconstructed a portion of the second floor to build out the new staircase and add the twenty-six-foot-high adjacent window. What took its place is a sculpted stepping form that floats in a gentle curve above the floor as though lifted by the breeze. New outdoor views come with each step; light plays on the floor, creating crisp snapshots of sculptural forms. Wood floors were replaced with regal three-by-seven-foot white marble slabs.

Once the landscaping and interior plans were approved, in came the bulldozers to take up the tennis courts, kidney-shaped pool, and pebble-filled circular driveway. Jennifer's new entryway design introduced a dramatic bridge over a water pool, leading to a huge bronze front door—the perfect opening to the breathtaking interior.

In the back, the stucco fortress-like windows were obliterated and numerous glass sliders installed to open to a huge new stone loggia, where the original pool was once planted. Four wide, luxurious platforms of cascading steps lead to a sliver of emerald lawn ending at the new sixty-seven-foot-long pool.

The low, twenty-two-foot-long gas fire pit presents a pleasant glow to evenings by the pool. Completing the owner's private oasis is a separate guesthouse and cabana furnished with twin massage tables, lounge, gas fireplace, television, full kitchen and bar, and barbeque.

Opposite: The twenty-two-foot-long fire pit adds a bit of architectural mystique to the patio, and as the light of day decreases, its glow becomes more pronounced.

Above: The Zen-like serenity of the living room comes from its perfect balance: four identical gray suede couches, black lacquer end tables with matching lamps, twin coffee tables, and a modern interpretation of antique chandeliers. Bush-hammered Thassos marble brings texture, as does the bronze Hanneke Beaumont sculpture.

Above: The custom-built bar is convenient to the living room, audio-visual room, and movie-screening studio. Shelving is black lacquer, as is the top of the bar. A Sub Zero wine refrigerator is within reach. **Following pages:** The lounge, tucked away from the main flow, is a peaceful oasis with comfortable, masculine seating and a fireplace.

Above: The outdoor lounge area is perfect for entertaining, dining, and spur-of-the-moment meetings poolside. A black and white theme is introduced in the comfortable, clean-lined lounge chairs and furniture. Cushions are covered in terry-cloth cotton, so sinking into the couch after a swim is luxurious as well as practical.

Above: The staircase sweeps up two stories of glass, with light and shapes reflecting off the white marble floors. Jennifer commissioned a rock sculpture in black granite, a detail processing nature but also masculinity, says the designer. Rock sculpture in unexpected places is something Jennifer always brings into her room landscapes.

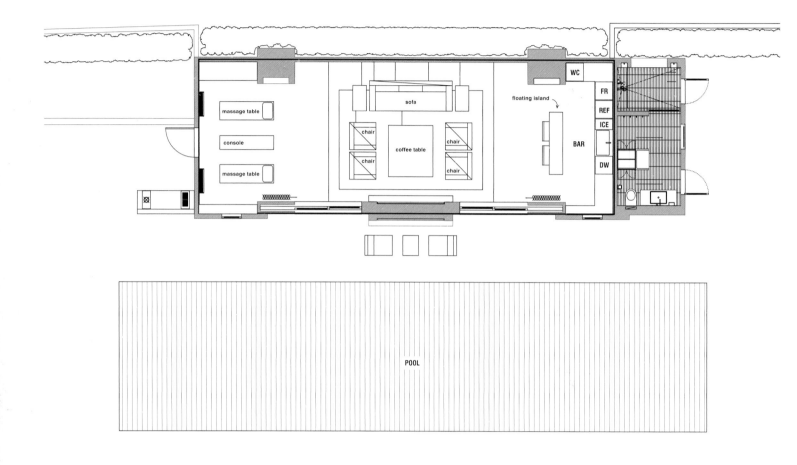

massage table

console

massage table

sofa

chair

chair

coffee table

chair

chair

floating island

WC

FR

REF

ICE

BAR

DW

POOL

Opposite: "The cabana was created so that my client could leave home for his daily massage, without ever really leaving home," says Jennifer. It's a comfortable little getaway, steps from the pool, with a lounge, full kitchen and bar, barbeque, and extra massage table for a guest who may like to share in the unwinding. **Following pages:** Starting with the solarium on the left, the entire back facade was transformed into a light-capturing rhythm of glass. The space flows easily to the patio and cabana.

ACKNOWLEDGMENTS

I want to express my gratitude to my clients, who trusted me to create their visions, and to all the talented contractors who made my creations possible. I would also like to thank my incredibly talented staff, the photographers who have shot my work, and the publications that have published my work over the years. And a special appreciation to Alex Tart of Rizzoli, Sam Shahid and Jonathan Caplan of Shahid & Company, and writer Anna Kasabian, who made this monograph possible.

Jennifer Post

Many thanks to my longtime editor, Alex Tart of Rizzoli, for embracing this concept and for bringing it together so beautifully; to Jennifer's amazing and supportive staff—Lena, Kyle, and Alison—for all of their help in keeping things flowing; to my dearest friend, Shawna Mullen, for always cheering me on and for her pearls of wisdom; and to David, my husband, for his support on this, my thirteenth book.

Anna Kasabian

Photography Credits Page 8-9: Stan Schnier; 10–11: Michael Moran; 12–29: Roger Davies; 30–43: Michael Moran and Antoine Bootz; 44–51: Stan Schnier; 52–63: Erhard Pheiffer; 64–75: Michael Moran; 76–87: Michael Moran and Antoine Bootz; 88–97: Antoine Bootz; 98–105: Antoine Bootz; 106–17: David Marlow; 118–35: Michael Moran; 136–51: Antoine Bootz; 152–67: Ken Hayden; 168–79: Ken Hayden; 180–89: Ken Hayden; 190–201: Michael Moran; 202–11: Michael Moran and Antoine Bootz; 212–23: Antoine Bootz; 224–37: Jennifer Post

First published in the United States of America in 2012 by Rizzoli International Publications, Inc.
300 Park Avenue South New York, NY 10010 www.rizzoliusa.com
© 2012 by Jennifer Post   text © 2012 by Anna Kasabian   Foreword © 2012 by Paige Rense

All rights reserved. No part of this publication may be reproduced, stored in a retrieval system,
or transmitted in any form or by any means, electronic, mechanical, photocopying, recording, or
otherwise, without prior consent of the publishers.

2012 2013 2014 / 10 9 8 7 6 5 4 3 2 1

Design by Sam Shahid

Distributed to the U.S. trade by Random House, New York
ISBN-13: 978-0-8478-3749-6
Library of Congress Control Number: 2011938529
Printed in China